Mrs. Houdini

UNIVERSITY OF CENTRAL FLORIDA PRESS

Contemporary Poetry Series

ORLANDO

Mrs. Houdini

POEMS BY

Rebecca McClanahan Devet

Library
University of Texas
at San Antonio

Library of Congress Cataloging-in-Publication Data

Devet, Rebecca McClanahan.
    Mrs. Houdini / Rebecca McClanahan Devet.
        p.   cm. — (University of Central Florida contemporary
  poetry series)
      ISBN 0–8130–0914–6 (alk. paper)
      I. Title. II. Title: Missus Houdini. III. Series.
  PS3554.E9274M77 1989
  811'.54—dc19   88–13884
                                            CIP

University Presses of Florida is the central agency for scholarly
publishing of the State of Florida's university system, producing
books selected for publication by the faculty editorial committees
of Florida's nine public universities. Orders for books published by
all member presses should be addressed to University Presses of
Florida, 15 NW 15th Street, Gainesville, Florida 32603.

Acknowledgments

Grateful acknowledgment is made to the following publications, where these poems previously appeared:

Carolina Quarterly: "Ancient Weaving" and "Produce Aisle"
Crucible: "She Wanted To Leave A Great Emptiness Behind" and "Evening Walk"
The Devil's Millhopper: "Water"
Emrys Journal: "Staining the Porch Rocker" and "Wednesday's Child"
The Lyricist: "Somewhere in Iowa, A Woman" and "Wendy"
Negative Capability: "Yes"
Nimrod: "Leah" and "Something Calling My Name"
Southern Poetry Review: "Snow Woman"
Wilmington Review: "The Word"

FOR MY SISTERS

Jennifer, Claudia, and Lana

Contents

But in a moment that which is behind naming makes itself known.

Susan Griffin, *Woman and Nature*

Snow Woman

In childhood's first flurry,
we never thought to build a woman.
Three small sisters

in woolen gloves, patting
together the perfectly
sexless, three-part man.

Stiff twig arms, the frozen smile.
Even Father's hat stolen from the shelf
did not make him ours.

Today in first snow
we are grown-up sisters
on our way to build a woman.

The oldest, stooped from sudden weight,
carries a daughter on her back.
The youngest carries hers in her belly.

What falls from the sky
is white and pure.
We catch it on our tongues.

If we could, we would build her whole.
Start at the head—pristine
features, a thoughtful nod.

But it can't be done. Our woman
requires a sturdy base.
Earth is the place to begin.

We pack the snow between
our hands, lower it to the ground,
gently roll it round.

Her body grows in our hands.
And as we roll, earth attaches itself—
twigs, branches, leaves.

We struggle, lift her upright in the snow,
kneel to carve the first space.
Her thighs spread wide,

we crawl on all fours
through the place where we began.
We pad more snow: the hills

of her buttocks. Too small a waist
and she would crumble,
we build her rounded there.

Together our hands do the work.
The breasts we build are Mother's breasts.
Shoulders broad, back strong.

And now the neck, the stem we pray
will hold. Tomorrow she will be gone,
yet we fashion her head as if

she were forever. Grandmother's
mouth, full lips and laughing.
The nose of our dead sister.

And for her eyes, an aunt
we never knew except in stories.
They say one eye was brown,

fixed straight ahead or slightly down.
The other was blue with a mind of its own,
gazing a bit toward heaven.

One

Ancient Weaving: The Mistress to the Wife

Each evening I knit him back to you.
As long as I am here, he will never
forget the way home. You dream yourself

Penelope, me the island woman, but see
how the years unravel in my hands
as he tells me the story, remembering

the long-ago curve of your neck
beneath the lamp, the child
woven into the fold of your arm.

I nod in his direction, my fingers
on the photograph he shows:
you in the kitchen, bending to carve

the meat, lean and rare as the body
you think I serve him. But come closer,
watch as he opens my robe, it falls

to the floor and my breasts, powdery,
heavy as yours, catch in the net
of his hands as they move to my thighs,

an old story he reads, remembering
you, me, the ancient seam
of what you most fear,

of what you are sure will be satin
and dark. If you look
it will stun you. The bed's whiteness,

the wind-fresh cotton I've folded
with hands like a mother's
that stroke him, counting each leap

of his pulse till I sleep
and dream I curl in the rim of the saucer
that cradles the teacup you hand him each night.

Leah

"Leah was tender eyed; but Rachel was beautiful and well favored.
And Jacob loved Rachel."
Genesis 29: 17–18A

I was the seven-year trick
my father played on Jacob.
I lay alone in the wedding tent,
heard the men, heavy with feasting,
leading him in darkness. He entered,
calling my sister's name, and in that moment
I knew being oldest was not enough.
I stared through the split
ceiling of the tent, counting stars
like unborn sons, my birthright swallowed
whole. Outside, the lowing of Father's cattle,
the cattle that would never be mine.
Yet all was not lost. For as it is written,
God looked down. And though Jacob
whispered Rachel's name, it was in me
his seed took root, flowering into Reuben.
In the morning Jacob turned to see
I was not the one. His eyes,
the cry that crawled from the pit
of his throat: *Rachel! Where is Rachel?*

Of course you have heard the story,
but it is always Jacob's. How he
saw her that day, his beautiful cousin,
leading sheep to the well. How he
kissed her, wept at the sudden love,
and in that moment bartered his life,
to lie with her. Seven years he labored,
was cheated on the bargain, only
these goods in return. The oldest daughter
must marry first: it all comes down to wages.
Again, the birthright law, the knot

he could not untie. Of all men,
Jacob should have known. Jacob, the twin,
who swam the womb in second place,
clutching the heel of his brother.
He should have remembered the tricks
of darkness, like the one he played
on his blind father, wrapping himself
in animal fur to steal his brother's blessing.

The years stirred between us. Seven more
he worked for her. And how many nights,
lying beneath him as he whispered her name,
I wanted to call out *Esau! I want your brother
Esau! The firstborn, your father's favorite.
The hairy one, the hunter!* But I kept
the peace. Spat out sons in rhythm,
my name as lost to him as that
one wild seed that sprouted Dinah,
the daughter he never counted.

There is much I cannot forgive,
but this comes closest: I lost my Rachel.
Before he came, how we loved each other!
Small sisters laughing, digging in dirt,
we played the magic of mandrake:
purple flower, love charm. We fingered
the forked root and guessed the shapes
of our husbands. And late night in the tent
we shared, we wondered at their names.

Then Jacob came. We lay alone in separate
tents, praying *Me tonight! Me!*
We locked our legs about him
like a prize, practiced how to keep him.
Sons, the only coin to spend.
We even gave our handmaidens to lie with him.
From my maiden, two sons. From hers,
two more. Rachel gave only the last two,
Jacob's favorites, sons of his old age.

He made Joseph a many-colored coat.
And Benjamin, bursting from Rachel's womb,
was welcomed in triumph, though he took
her last breath. Twelfth son!
Now Israel could begin, a country
torn from the loins of two sisters.

Long ago God promised Jacob's seed
would be as the dust of the earth.
I did my part. Count them.
Listen to their names:
Reuben, Simeon, Levi, Judah.
Issachar and Zebulum. Half the tribes of Israel.
When Jacob looked at me, he saw sons,
the flowering of a new nation.
I was Leah, but I was more.
I only wanted to be Leah.
And I might have forgiven it all
if I had seen written in his eyes,
even once, my name.

Water

For over a year, a retired schoolteacher in California has watered her lawn night and day, even in the rain. Although her bill averages $300 a month and city officials threaten to cut off her flow, she refuses to stop watering.

Charlotte Observer

I crawled my mother's womb on cracked knees,
the green memory of fins and gills still wet in my mind.

My childhood was a tunnel of flannel, my father
a desert of needle and spine, but for years I believed

the legend: even a cactus contains a lake.
His last words rattled, husks in his throat.

My husband was a silent land. Strong, I thought,
believing again. I dug deep for forty years, through

the stone and shale of his touch. I never struck water.
I came close with the children, hundreds

of students lined up and thirsty. I poured myself out.
Now at night I dream them, slumped over dry desks,

chapped hands folded, their lips split and bleeding,
still begging stories. It's just not right.

Three-fourths of earth covered with water and me
with a cough I can't raise. You'd think my body

would give some up, that with nine-tenths of myself
bubbling streams, I'd get some relief. The neighbors

curse the sidewalk pools, puddles seeping beneath
their porches, algae creeping the driveways.

The city men come tomorrow to cut the fittings
and leave just a trickle. But I'll find a way.

Last night when I washed the dishes, I flooded
the floor, ankle-happy. Forget the ark.

Let the waters rise and cleanse us till we drown.
Grass can never be too green.

Something Calling My Name

There are times when I really miss it.
I wish I had some dirt right now.

Fannie Glass, a clay-eater, who has been off dirt for
over a year, at her husband's request.

I try to tell him. But he won't hear.
Earl, I say, it's safe, it's clean
if you dig below where man has been,
deep to the first blackness.
I tell him. But he won't hear.
Says my mouth used to taste like mud,
made him want to spit.

I try to tell him how fine it was.
When I was big with Earl Junior and Shad,
I laid on my back, my belly all swelled
like the high dirt hills
sloping down to the bank
above the gravel road by Mama's.
And I'd dream it. Rich and black after rain.
Like something calling my name.

I say Earl, remember? That spring in Chicago,
I thought I'd die, my mouth all tasteless,
waiting for Wednesdays, shoeboxes
full of the smell of home.
The postman, he'd scratch his head,
but he kept on bringing. Bless Mama.
She baked it right, the way I like.
Vinegar-sprinkled. And salt.
I'd carry it in the little red pouch
or loose in my apron pocket
and when the day got too long and dry
and Earl home too late for loving,
I'd have me a taste. It saved me, it did.
And when we finally made it back,
the smell of Alabama soil

poured itself right through me.
I sang again and things were fine
till the night he leaned back and said
No More, his man-smells all rich
and mixed up with evening. Right there,
laying by me, he made me choose
between his kisses and my clay.

Now afternoons when it gets too much,
I reach for the stuff he gave me.
Baking soda. Starch. I've tried it all.
But I don't hold with it.
It crunches good, but it's all bleached out
and pasty. It just don't take the place.

Earl, I say, I've given it up.
And right then, I have.
But sometimes on summer nights like this
when the clouds hang heavy
and I hear that first rumble and the earth
peels itself back and the crust darkens
and the underneath soil bubbles up
damp and flavored, it all comes back
and I believe I'd do anything
to kneel at that bank
above the gravel road by Mama's
and dig in deep till my arms are smeared
and scoop it wet to my mouth.

Somewhere in Iowa, a Woman

The dark smell takes her back.
She leans over steaming pots,
the soft flesh of plums,
skins slipping off in her hands.
She stares as if steam holds the answer
and once released could heal.
Her hair clings damp, curling
on her cheek like a woman giving
birth all over again. Her breath
fogs the window. She calls their names.
Her daughters, years gone.

From faded pictures, Mona,
her name dark honey
poured across the tongue.
When they told her, she kept right on
sprinkling each tiny dress.
The iron hissed in nests
of small puffed sleeves.
She pressed lace collars,
finished, untied her apron.
Stacked the dresses, flat and dry,
at the end of the ironing board.

And Deborah. Horses pulled the wagon,
plow horses harnessed to a lighter task,
this wooden casket that might have been
a tool box, but nothing inside rattled.
In a flannel gown she stood by the window,
watching the awkward horses pass,
their breath frozen silver on the muzzles.

The Test

*Proofs of witchcraft include additional breasts, inability to weep,
marks of the devil, and failure in the water test.*

You say I sour milk, keep butter from setting.
Children collapse in my arms. The devil, you say,
I know him well. Toads and weasels are my familiars.
You strip me, searching a hive of breasts, then prick
my flesh for the final sign: a mark you say I cannot feel.

Tomorrow is the water test. If I'm guilty,
I'll stay afloat. Innocent, I sink. Either way I lose,
like the long ago woman in Zittau, six hours underwater,
stuffed in a sack with a rooster, a viper, a cat,
while above on dry land the choirboys sang
    Aus tiefer Noth schrei ich zu Dir.
    Out of great trouble I cry to thee.

I cried the first time on the ducking stool
and later in the cage where you pelted me with jeers
and rotted stumps. You say I rouse storms,
split open the sky for rain, but when you led me
through the streets like a disobedient horse,
I could squeeze no tears. Today I watched my sister ignite,
her hair a flaming radiance while her accuser
stood by, the payment jingling in his pocket.

Wendy

" . . . the window blew open as of old, and Peter dropped on the
floor. He was exactly the same as ever, and Wendy saw at once that
he . . . was a little boy and she was grown up. She huddled by the
fire . . . squeezing herself as small as possible. Something inside
her was crying, 'Woman, woman, let go of me.' "

from J. M. Barrie's *Peter Pan*

I thought he would always return
each April, spring-cleaning time,
to fly me to the place where young
is everything and always,
like the first time I woke to his cries,
this boy hunting his shadow.
He was dressed in skeleton leaves and berries,
smelling of juices that ooze from trees.
How could I not love him?
I found the shadow where Mother left it,
folded in the bureau. I stitched it back
and flew with him out the window
to the forest where the lost boys waited
my apron, my needle, the stories I could tell.

All those years of redskins and beasts,
mermaids and one-armed pirates.
All those years of stitching pockets.
I grew tired. He forgot my name.
The April he did not return, I waited
by the window. My dress of berries and leaves
drew tight across my breasts.
I tugged at the hem and wished myself gone
or squeezed like Tinkerbell
to a fist of light, forever small.
That is when Mother told me:
I was not the first.
Long ago she knew him too,
and though he soon forgot her name,
for years her heart was a puzzle

of boxes, the innermost shut tight,
and still she wears a kiss
on the corner of her mouth
meant for Peter.

Now a daughter sleeps in my bed.
I stitch by the nursery window.
A breeze lifts the curtains and I know
he has wandered back again, worn
from all that adventure and light
and everlasting childhood.
My daughter stirs and I search the darkness
till I find the shadow, draped
carelessly at the foot of her bed.
I hold it close and dance,
then fold it neatly into the bureau,
as mothers do.

A Simple Woman

"A weak woman must have the courage
To accept what she is . . . .
A simple woman, that's me."

Fumiko Kimura

Distraught over what she considered her failure as wife and
mother, Fumiko Kimura followed the tradition of oya-ko-shinju, an
ancient Japanese practice of parent-child suicide. The
once-promising pianist waded into the sea off Santa Monica,
California, with her two children.

I kneel and stroke
his slender feet.
How white they are,
adrift in the water.
The bowl is clean
and blue as the sea
that stretches to Japan,
to my mother and sisters
whose voices call me.
All a wife has to do
is love her husband
and be ready
to open at his touch.
His lover's breasts
are petals.

Daughter Kuri tugs at me,
never enough milk.
And the music room is bare,
the piano hid away
from Kazutaka.
Now he will not bump his head,
pinch his fingers in the keys.
I would not be
oni no you nà hito,
demon mother who leaves
her children behind.

So when the ocean calls,
I take them too,
their arms about my neck.
The sand is soft.
Together, our footprints
deeper than my own.

She Wanted to Leave a Great Emptiness Behind

In the house she would leave all the fullness
she could stir: sauces bubbling, white tents
of bread rising in the pan. Peonies perfect
in the vase and below, the polished oak.
Cushions plumped, his brandy poured, coating
the petalled glass. And she would leave
her garden in all its wildness: fence vines
climbing the difficult ascent, purple
tangle of morning glory, so it might seem
it all thrived greener where her hands had been.

Then in the swell of the moment she would be gone,
leaving the great emptiness. And regret
would pile deep in his lap as plums.
And when he steered mourners through the halls
bare with her absence, he would mumble
but when she was here, and they would nod.

Do not question why she wanted this.
Truth is the strange cat outside our door
that will not come in lest we name him
and soften his color with our cream.
That is the way with truth, our mouths
on the thermos cannnot see, only taste
the sweet or bitter when blind it enters
our throats. To spill is to waste its secret.
And departure wears its own perfume, aging
as it is born: doilies yellowed at the edge,
peonies bowing, fine talcum of dust.
Even the white mites fluttering the blossoms
could be her kiss. Together perhaps they wrote
this ending. Or some other hand floating
the spaces between. It could be worse.
Recall the warm socket when a tooth is gone.

You tongue the bruise, remembering.
So in the garden finally he might know her
as he sits alone on the marble bench.
Moss on the cherubs weaves a shawl
and even the smallest rose dying
leaves a cavern rain hollows out,
where roots once made their bed.

Mrs. Houdini

"Houdini hasn't come. I don't believe he will."
Bess Houdini, as she switched off the light by her
husband's portrait, after waiting ten years past his
death for his spirit to speak.

Your trick was the longest,
to wait out those years
cuffed to his memory:
King of Magic,
Undisputed Monarch of Shackles
who slithered from slave collars,
melted through walls
while you stood beside him, smiling.

It started with a vanishing act—
first date, Coney Island.
He waved his arms,
you fled your girlhood
and in the flurry, dropped your name.
You were just what he needed,
a petite soubrette,
stockings wrinkling at the knees,
the buckled dancing shoes.
A slip of a thing,
ninety-four pounds.
How well you fit in the box.

And when his public demanded more,
the playbill artist painted
breasts, hips. Stroke by stroke,
curve by curve,
you changed into Mrs. Houdini.

Metamorphosis, his favorite act,
featured ropes, sack, and a trunk.
In a three-second switch

you slid from yourself,
became him, jacket and all.
But the time he lost the key,
how was it then, inside the trunk,
listening for the click?
The audience stirred,
leaned in their seats
while you waited,
the clock ticking,
your small feet thumping,
your breath closing in.
Of course he made it.
Always, just in time
to take his bow.

And when he vanished,
you were still here,
real as the coffin hermetically sealed,
real as the earth he denied.
Beneath his portrait you sat silent,
his old letters in your lap,
waiting his spirit's return
until the night
you switched off the light,
his heavy name
dropped from your shoulders,
and light as a girl,
you bobbed to the surface
tasting the air
while all around
the waves wove a chant—
Bess, Bess—
the spell of your natural name.

Two

The Seven Wives of Zeus

1. Metis, Goddess of Wisdom

There's little to tell. I taught
him all I knew, caught
as I was in the glare
of his mantle, the waving hair,
the bolt of thunder
in his hand. It's too late to wonder
why he took this blessing I bore
and turned it on me. They say I knew more
than all the gods of heaven
and earth, that even
Zeus with his sceptre and crown
of oak leaves, would bow down
to my children. So as my time
drew near, we played our game
of changing shapes, and when I grew small
as a fly, he swallowed me whole
and with it my power
till I was no more
than a tiny voice
whispering advice
from the pit of his belly
where inside of me
Athene grew—my first
and only daughter—grew till she burst,
not as a child wet from my womb,
but from the wound
of his head, wielding a sword,
a woman full grown and armored.

2. Themis, Goddess of Order

Mine was never the name
he called out in sleep. Too tame
perhaps. No fire from my eyes,
no clever disguise
like snakes for hair. Mine was always arranged
in the same wave, unchanged
one harmonious day
to the next. That was my way.
Once I owned the oracles.
I gave them up to wear the scales
of order. Like clockwork I planned
the four children I claim:
Justice, the Seasons, Legislation, Peace.
The cock-eyed Fates were *his*
idea, crazy daughters engendered
one night as I slept. I remembered
too late his power to slide
into other skin, to hide
in a shower of gold,
a pigeon's wing, a cloud.
I knew what he wanted: to dally
all night with mortals, nymphs, the wild eye
glancing. He flirted with Chance,
but in the sanity of day it was balance
he chose. So while he was out gathering
clouds, I stayed by the hearth preparing
feasts, the golden nectar
I served the gods long after
the Lord of winds and thunder
left, searching elements stormier.

3. Eurynome, Goddess of All Things

Who could love him better
than I? Universal Mother, Daughter
of the Old Ocean. Naked I rose from chaos,
danced alone on the waves till Boreas,
the North Wind, blew his seed
into me and I brooded like a bird, laid
the egg which held it all: stars, planets, moon,
even the sky where Zeus himself was born.
Wide-Wandering was my name,
Exalted Dove. And so one night Zeus came
and stayed. Our daughters
were the Graces,
most lovely nymphs found
in earth and sea. But that is not what bound
him to me those long years. Perhaps it was
my mermaid tail, the silver scales
I wrapped around him as he swam
like a child in the curve of my arm.
Perhaps it was my ocean
taste, the salt they say men
remember and swim to all their lives.
I always knew he would take other wives,
but being the original giver,
I forgave. Now they call me Lethe, river
of forgetfulness. That is not so.
Each night without him I begin the slow
crawl back to the waves, the darkness
where long ago he found me. And in this wetness
I search for him, over and over,
not knowing if what I seek is husband, son, or lover.

4. Demeter, Goddess of Earth

My life did not begin
with his touch, nor with the mortal Iasion,
though we lay together in a thrice-plowed
field till Zeus, passing in a cloud,
saw us there and wanted that heat.
Secretly every man wants a woman with dirt
on her hands, a woman bent over a plow,
sowing the empty furrow.
Yes, Zeus was lusty, nearly my match.
Together from our thrones we would watch
the flocks below as they drifted
on the hills. Till bored with godliness, we shifted
shapes, I a mare and he a bull.
We were both at home in the animal.
I might have stayed there always, the corn goddess
stripped willingly of her crown, barley princess
forever young. I did not know the seed
of a daughter would sprout and feed
that hollow place. But from our union
Kore was born and Love opened its thousand
blossoms. From that day on
I was Mother and life began.
And Zeus who knew all, knew that. One
nod to his brother Hades and she was gone,
sucked to the world below where Kore
became Persephone,
wife of darkness. You know the rest.
You call it a happy ending, the daughter lost
now found, how Zeus finally gave in
to my cries so the dying earth would live again,
but to me there is no victory
when every autumn I lose her to a husband, bury
my treasure in the ground,
the same soil where once I found
my life in *her.* When you've lost your daughter,
what does it matter that the whole earth calls you Mother.

5. Mnemosyne, Goddess of Memory

Some say I was soon
forgotten, a breeze blown
in and gone. Some call me whore,
but I gave him a choir
of daughters,
nine muses,
one for each night he lay
with me. And in them my memory
lives, in the bruise of remembrance,
the winged dance,
the song
sweetly sung,
the harmony
and dark prophecy
of what will come.
Weavers of sleep and oblivion,
we enter the loose seam
of night, and in his dream
we stir our feathers
till he wakes and remembers
I was there at the start.
And he learns me by heart.

6. Leto, Goddess of Night

Come closer. I will teach
you how to see in the dark. Reach
and feel how smooth the skin
that has never known sun.
Lift the veil and see the face
Zeus loved. The way you trace
your own shadow
climbing the walls of a cave, that is how
he loved me. But the others
called me Bad Luck Goddess
and sent me to birth our
twins alone, this double seed whose power
they feared. Cities closed their bright
doors. No place bathed in light
would claim me. Nine nights I labored
and would have carried
them forever, but Zeus sent Poseidon
in mercy to the island
where I hid. To shade me
he fashioned over my head a watery
dome. I clutched a palm tree
in my arms. My knees
pressed hard against the earth
till Artemis burst forth
and then the ground below
smiled as from my loins Apollo
leapt, clothed in the white linen
of day, most dazzling god shot through with sun.

7. Hera, Goddess of Marriage

Other men? I could have had them all.
Meteors ripen in the fold of my veil.
I'm Queen Of The Sky! The Milky Way
is the milk I spilled one day
as I suckled my child. Yes, hundreds of men!
More than the peacock eyes of Argus. (Once Ixion
embraced a cloud, thinking it was I.)
But from the beginning I set my eye
on *him*, the god of luminous ether.
I rule the lower, denser
air. We were meant for each other.
Don't even bother
counting other wives. I've blinded men for less.
(Ask Tiresias.)
You've heard us clattering about heaven,
throwing our weight around, his uneven
thunder, the zigzag revolt
of the lightning bolt
he slings at my crown. That's just his way
of loving me. You can say
what you will, a man wants an equal,
not a sequel
to himself. So understand this:
These chains on my wrists,
the iron bracelets, the anvils
on my ankles
can't hold me! Besides, I like this view.
It's all in the way you
look at it. Hanging upside-down
is not so bad, as long as your crown
stays put. It's staying power
that matters, from the first hour
on, past dragons and mistresses, past
disobedient children, you last,
live out all your lives with him:
Girl. Wife. Old Woman.

Three

First Lessons

*. . . the two most powerful words in the infant-room vocabulary,
under any circumstances: ghost, kiss . . .*
Sylvia Ashton-Warner, who taught kindergarten to
the Maori tribe of New Zealand

These small ones tell it.
How the spirit
hovering Daddy's bed
lifts its head
and the kiss
Mommy plants like a moth
on their eyes each night
is white
and smells of death.

We teachers hush them,
move on to our lessons.
But already they know
how it comes. And even
as we turn to our books,
they mumble *ghost, kiss.*

Evening Walk

The children in my neighborhood
leave themselves on sidewalks,
their silhouettes drawn in chalk
the way police mark victims
exactly as they fall. They could be
my childhood paper dolls,
the ones I cut so carefully,
turning the blunt scissors
each difficult curve, respecting
the slim necks
and what one slip would mean.

In Beirut children dream shells and cannons,
believing the butterflies are dead.
And I remember the slant-eyed girl aflame
who once ran naked through
the six o'clock news, her arms reaching.
This evening I step as if treading
some sacred ground, though I know
as my eyes trace the outlines,
these are the ones who got away.
This one, hearing her mother's call,
peeled herself free of the pavement.
And this one simply stood and walked,
Lazarus bursting the bonds of
his graveclothes and moving
toward his astonished sisters.

I smell the sweetness of autumn fires
from chimneys that promise evening
after evening of children asleep
in fathers' laps. In Auschwitz
chimneys burned with the flesh of the young,
the chosen ones, thin as lost promises,
too weak to lift a finger
as Hansel was asked to do.

I walk and darkness settles.
Light blossoms in windows.
Inside, the children soften and fatten.
Tonight they have somehow slipped
through the bars, past the finger pointing.
Do I shout thanksgiving? To whom
do I bow? What sacrifice bring?
I remember how the near-sighted witch
caged the boy, fed him to bulging.
And when the day came, Hansel,
grown fat on goose liver,
pressed a chicken bone through the bars
and stalled the terrible dinner.

Wednesday's Child

He is the one who knows
only one crayon,
who sits in shadows
scribbling stormclouds,
defending gray
which he knows is silver
with the shine rubbed off.
Each night Mother offers
Humpty Dumpty rhymes
and the pillow of her lap,
not knowing when she closes
the door, how the story explodes,
how the clumsy Egg Man topples
and the child's chest
splits like an egg
and yellow fear
splatters the walls
until dolls squeal
his name in rubber chorus.
Soon the child will catch
the scent of a whiskered wolf
loose in the woods.
He will run and run
the tangled path
and there will be
no crumbs to follow.

Sestina

FOR THE KITTENS

Beside the bed made from a box, I pause
to watch you crawl the hill of your mother
who lies exhausted on the old sheet stained
with blood, beside the dark sister
of afterbirth she is eating to nourish
what is left of herself. You are a litter

of five I thought I could do without, litter
the world had enough of. Another bundle of paws
and whiskers, more pink mouths to nourish
in a world already full. *Sometimes the mother
cat knows. Some eat their young,* whispers my sister
beside me and I imagine the cat's mouth stained

with her kittens' blood. The image stains
my memory: Mother carried on a litter
by nuns who tell Father another brother or sister
will be born to take her place. He pauses
and cannot speak. My mother
opens her eyes to nourish

the silence. Inside her, the dark cake nourishes
the child struggling to get out. The sheet is stained
with birth's first blood and Mother
lies quietly. Pain lights her
eyes and Father reaches, paws
the air as nurses roll her away. Later my sister

surprises them all, turns on her own. The Sister
in nurse's white enters the waiting room, nourished
suddenly by her voice. I look up. Pause.
I stare at the blood, stained
on her cuff. She opens her mouth, her announcement littering
the air: *You have a sister. And a mother*

too. It surprises most my mother
who wakes expecting heaven, sees instead my sister
wet and squirming on the litter
of sheets like these where I watch you suck, nourished
by warm milk and I know this world is not stained
enough with kittens. Your small lives pause

before me. I am not your mother. There's little nourishment
here. But like an expectant sister I wait, stained
and eager for the litter of new eyes, your padded paws.

The Wreck

The sky unrolled like a ribbon
that afternoon, and we had to go
out to the field behind our house
where we chased the children
through tall grass.
Minutes passed as they do
till something squealed a warning
and we turned past ourselves
to the fence where a truck
leapt the highway and landed
in the tree at the edge of our field.
Then the horn we would hear
nights after in our sleep. You ran
to the phone. I stayed with the children
and could not stop looking,
like those people I'd always hated,
rubberneckers who slow to stare.
And worse. I moved closer.

Sirens throbbed and workers gathered
and the saw sharpened its teeth
on the metal and tree now grown together,
to reach the ones inside, the flesh pulsing
in the shell like a baby's soft spot.
I knew you were waiting for me, for the children
to join you on safe ground,
but I held tight to their hands
(*so you won't blow away*, I said,
in the helicopter wind) for already we heard
the whunk-whunk of its blades and our hair
stood on end like the moment
before lightning. The tall grass
parted and the helicopter
set down like a water strider.

From its belly two figures in white
ran with their bags to the tree where a blond head
emerged through the twisted chrome.
High as a hero they lifted him, the stretcher
floating the grass. His feet hung
over the edge, a child too large for this bed.
The next one came quick as a second twin,
they slid him into the van.
Then everything slowed.
From somewhere a white sheet, and I knew
with this one they would take their time.
An old man turned to me. Through yellow teeth
he squeezed each word: *There's a dead one there,*
something like pride in his voice.
I looked down at the children. It would be months
before I wondered what they saw that day.
I stood holding their warm hands,
then turned toward you,
wading the tall grass home.

Neighborhood Fire

Blue lights and sirens like midnight prowlers
enter dozens of bedrooms and for a moment
we all dream the same dream, then one by one rouse

to stare through windows where women in bathrobes
move to get a closer look. Slippers brush the sidewalk
like pastel feather dusters and husbands

in boxer shorts occupy the porches, their children,
in the habit of circuses and parades, lifted high
on their shoulders. The widow's house is burning,

but we cannot locate the flame. Only smoke,
black smoke leaking from windows
we thought well sealed. Firemen prowl the dark,

flashlights arc-ing over the lawn.
They search for accustomed drama,
leap and crackle of their trade, something

to put their hoses to. The widow stands watching.
We have caught her half-dressed, breasts loose
beneath a cotton gown, her hair a white surprise.

She crosses her arms as if to say,
"Haven't you seen enough?"
Yet still we stare, shake our heads and mutter,

clutching the cool columns that hold our houses up.
Hoses coil snugly on clean red trucks. We yawn.
So slow a burn we turn away. Children slide

from fathers' arms, women scuff back to their houses.
The widow sees it all through a smoky blur, remembers
the bedside table, glasses folded on the open book.

Tomorrow the agent will estimate the damage.
She watches the firetrucks pull away. Her feet
are pink and childish against the dark grass.

Produce Aisle

The artichoke keeps her distance.
She has been taken too many times. Now
the armadillo armor hides her secret heart.

Everyone counts on the onion, staple of stews
and pottage. But deep in the crowded bin, her skin
is thin as moth wing. It peels away before their eyes.

Green peppers are modern women who take
their muscles seriously. They hunch their shoulders,
broad, shiny beneath a fluorescent sun.

Close by in cellophane the carrots keep for weeks,
the last to lose their figures. All legs,
tapering to slim ankles—and above,

wild profusion of hair. They gather in knots
of conversation and whisper about the apples,
those aging showgirls who didn't know when to quit,

redheads buffed an unnatural blush, a shine
that shouts *forever* while inside the white flesh softens.
In the center aisle, bananas in bunches

curl like firm young girls in sleep. Soon they will turn
like their half-price sisters, learn the bruise,
dark print that begins beneath the skin and grows.

Oh to be the avocado! She ages so well.
Time makes love to her daily, finding her sweeter
the softer she grows. Beside her the potato,

peasant woman in brown, comes into her own slowly.
She stays in the shadows, blindly remembers
her place. *Come to me! I will make you whole!*

coos the eggplant mother. And from the corner bin
a chorus: *Oranges, Oranges, Oranges, Oranges.*
We are what we seem. We speak our own name.

One Flesh

Even in this spoon-cradle
of sleep, his sex
pressed warm against you,

even in the near-perfect
curve of a couple
grown almost into one,

there is this: the extra elbow,
the arm with no home.
Where do you put it?

Do you leave it here,
beneath your head, till it falls
asleep, wakes heavy, tingling,

and you stare at it,
willing the fingers to move
as if they belonged to a stranger?

They say it is possible,
the perfect arc, two merging
flawlessly to one.

So for a moment you wish
it gone, this offending limb
with a mind of its own.

Why not fold it gently
into the bureau, between
the handkerchiefs and gowns

and dream the rest:
knuckles and knees
slide from their sockets

one by one.
This his too. Ankles,
elbows, shoulder blades, spines,

rise from your bodies
and stack themselves
white and glistening

beneath the window.
Basted with moonlight,
your bones and his,

while across the room
the two of you curl
boneless and soft,

becoming the other
like Bible couples
they told you about:

one flesh.
And you the wife: forsaking
all others, cleaving to him.

Visit with the Newlyweds

She does not know how white her neck,
or how naked. He cannot pass her
without touching. It is summer,
their cotton clothes soft as gauze.
The relatives have given gifts
they will grow into. China teacups.
Glass birds. A clock with a second hand.
I have brought Sweet Williams.
She is amazed something so pink
can bloom every year without planting.
Yes, I answer. *Eleven years for us.*
Eleven? she asks and looks at the clock
as if everything were told in hours.
Upstairs by their bed, the wedding pillow.
Every night they marry again.
I want to tell them how crowded
the bed will become, how soon
he will sleep with her mother.
The bride yawns, her eyes
turning back the sheet.
Back home the sheets are thin,
the roses worn smooth
beneath bodies so familiar
we wear our skin like clothes.
You touch me and I move to lower
the straps I pretend are there.
Some nights I forget we are married.
Some nights it is all I know.

Knowing How My Suns Die

We argued all night
and into morning
which I called *next*
but you called simply *morning.*
No such thing as endings, you said.
Everything is round, repeats itself,
so when you see a bird
disappear into the west
if you sit in that place
long enough, watchful,
you will see the same bird
emerge in the east,
like the sun.

Speaking of birds, I interrupted.
You call them free
but if you're right
they are caught
in their closet of blue
doomed forever to move their wings,
never stopping, not even to mate.
And, back to suns, I continued.
I have always believed
every sun is new,
birthed red in the east each morning,
stretching its life across the sky
to die in the west that night.
I have always believed what I see.

Then you called me Columbus,
threw back your head
and laughed my ignorance to the ceiling
where I said it falls
to the carpet to die
but you said it lives, reverberating,
bouncing back, floor to ceiling

to floor, always alive
in the spaces I cannot
reach with my hands.
No, I argued, shaking my head.
I have always believed what I see.

So when you left
I cried, *Don't go,*
knowing how my suns die.
I watched you turn, and the laughter
you threw over your shoulder
I prayed would bounce from you
to me to you.
And I have sat in this place
so long. Wanting so to be wrong.
I sit still, try to feel
the dizziness there must be
if it's true,
if we are truly spinning
and it's all one, all true
that we spin back
like your one sun,
the one you swear always returns.

Staining the Porch Rocker

I would have left it as it was.
Pale, newly shaven.
Nails poking their heads
through the innocent pine.
The sun would have bleached it
to buckling, the rains
softened it to destruction,
a sweet rotting where ants
and termites make their home.
I have always been one
to love a natural aging.

But you left too soon,
and alone that night
I found a dozen reasons.
My hands were bare.
The stain oily, thick.
I stroked the arms,
the hard back, the slats
driven fast together.
Even the spaces beneath,
the spaces no one sees,
I rubbed,
my hands on the bare wood
darkening.

Angels

FOR MY SISTER

Only an angel fresh from a fall
would know how far we have come
from that summer when the sky
forgot to open, nothing above our heads
but sleek plastic tubes that fed your heart.
And me like Jacob beside you,
my head on a stone pillow.
Ninety times I changed the needle
and slipped it into your veins,
watching you sleep, your skin's pallor.
Night by night I practiced
how to give you up.
I would empty you from my arms
and fill the space with your daughter,
the baby I rocked and made my own.
But when I held her, it was you I saw,
thirty years ago. I was still on tiptoe,
watching through the slats of your crib,
waiting your next breath.

The angel of Ezekiel had four faces:
lion, ox, eagle, man, and the feet of a grazing calf.
They say the first angels were wingless,
like distant cousins visiting, no trumpets.
Of the nine heavenly choirs,
only the lowliest touch us.
Their name means messenger.
And that summer I would have smeared
the doorway with my blood
to keep that angel from his errand,
the message I heard in the dark.

I have seen museum angels
reaching out with all they have left,
stumps and hollow sockets.
The years have worn their faces smooth.
It might be any eyes here—
your daughter, our grandmother
looking down. Those nights by your bed,
smoothing the linen,
I tried to call back those faces,
remembering the halo Mother made,
how she twisted wire to a circle
while Father bent a coat hanger into wings
that he strapped on my back for the pageant
where I was the smallest angel
singing Midnight Clear.
The straps dug into my back.
That is what I remembered

until you touched me from the bed,
your eyes lit
as if from the sky's reflection.
I turned to see the stone rolled away
like Mary, bearing spices for the dead,
who walked past the risen one,
thinking he was the gardener.
Surrounded by seraphim hosts of light,
she walked right past.

First Signs

Some women know by the blue light
of the refrigerator, having
woken begging
just the right

answer. The cool compartments welcome.
Here pickles
float in dark juices
and cheeses age on their own.

Some know it by touching
themselves. All over the world
women curled
into the backs of sleeping

husbands. Some learn
through a knowing stranger.
The plump, pink nurse reads their
early morning urine,

cheerfully phones the results.
Congratulates. Always, no
matter what. Some know
it first through absence,

missing what they counted on:
twenty-eight, twenty-nine, forty-two, forty-three.
They check the cotton panel, see
how white it stays. The moon goes on

without them. Some never know, the child
lost somewhere in fleshy
folds like the fat woman rushing
to the hospital, wild

with pain. She named it
Appendicitis. One hour later,
delivered a screaming, red-faced baby.
Some try to forget

the question.
A child on each sleeve unravels.
Then one day a skirt tumbles
free of mothballs. She tugs it on,

it stretches tight and the question
asks itself. And maybe some
lucky ones glimpse it first in dream,
the child tucked in the soft quilted

brain, between layers of *chance* and *wanting*.
Slowly the child unwraps the gauze
of its mother's eyes
and the woman wakes new, knowing.

Yes

Myrrh is not a gift for the living,
so why these burial beads
my mother sends, thinking of me?
The night I was planted in her,
the dirt was fresh on my sister's grave.
Her name was Sylvia. I have seen the gravestone
nudging its head through the Illinois field
toward an immensity of sky. Sky
is all she recalls of that day, sky
and plow horses through the gray snow
and how No was the only word she could form:
No to her children and No to her husband
and No to her own next day. How Yes crept in,
she cannot remember, but next summer
she sat in church in a black crepe
maternity dress and said Yes to something
and light sneaked through her white gloves
and beneath her hat and she named me Rebecca,
from the Bible, a month before I was born

and August loped in, heavy and hot
as their Irish setter with the one glass eye.
The day I was born she braided my living
sister's hair, walked my brother
to the outhouse and wiped him
and fed the chickens and milked the black cow.
She carried water in buckets
up steps from the spring house
to the stove, then down to the wringer washer
where dashers knocked, beating my father's
overalls clean. Two children at her knees
and one still rocking in her head,
and one in her belly pushing.

The Word

1. Daily Bread

With milk each morning,
I cried for my word,
mouth open to catch
the water Mother dropped
on my hungry tongue.
I watched her teeth, straight
and white as the words she gave.
Her lips closed, split apart,
her tongue flashed out
then suddenly in.
Light, she whispered,
tugging the switch up and down
till my eyes blinked in rhythm.
She taught me *water, saucer, yes.*
Shadow she would save.

Today I wake, hungry.
Say *grotto* to me, I beg.
You tease me with *seashell,*
starfish, crab. But I need *grotto,*
the grit on my teeth, the growl.
Last month it was *hollow.*
Everywhere I traced it.

2. In the Beginning

Here in this wind-swept cabin,
stripped of television and toys,
our daughters are making a language.
On their haunches they bend together
as if beside some ancient fire.
They rub their hands
and the first words spark:
Booca (bread). *Itsa* (I).

Hot. Cold. Hungry.
Soon they shiver, reach for *you*.
Join hands, dance circles.
Now a new hunger starts
deep in their throats:
a simple word for *song*.

3. Love's Language

Not flowers. Not the simple
picture our young son draws,
a rose opening soft as a sigh
to the lily's insistent pistil.
When you come
it is more like going
and you clutch me to tether yourself
to earth, swinging out, out
to the blackness of *in*.

4. Grandmother, after the Stroke

There was nothing left to say
after she called the porch a cemetery.
Her signals bred hybrids.
Now slippers are catacombs
and Ruth is Marge.

5. Voice Lesson

Somewhere you lost it
and must find it again,
the voice you were born with.
When the wind starts,
your strings will vibrate.
Now we will begin.
On your back.
Pant like a puppy
till your whole cage
Expands.   Contracts.   Expands.

You are a newborn,
cords of elastic,
chin loose as butter.
We will begin again.

Notes

"The Seven Wives of Zeus"

Sources differ markedly on the number of Zeus' wives and
the order of his marriages. Homer makes Hera the first wife of
Zeus and includes an eighth consort, Dione. However,
according to Hesiod, Zeus had seven wives in the order given
in this poem.

"Yes"

Myrrh, a sweet-smelling spice with a bitter taste, was one of
the gifts of the Magi to the infant Jesus. Later, this gift was
interpreted by many biblical scholars as a prophetic symbol of
Christ's suffering and death. The Egyptians used pulverized
myrrh for embalming purposes, and, in early Jewish custom,
myrrh was wrapped inside the linen burial clothes to protect
the body from rapid decomposition.

Photograph by Lana Rubright

REBECCA MCCLANAHAN DEVET, author of *Mother Tongue* (1987), has been poet-in-residence for Charlotte-Mecklenburg Schools since 1981. She has been nominated for a Pushcart prize and the CCLM General Electric Award for Younger Writers. Her poetry and fiction have been published widely, and she has edited several anthologies of children's poetry, including *I Dream So Wildly* (Briarpatch Press, 1986). She received her Ph.D. and M.A.T. from University of South Carolina and currently resides in Charlotte, North Carolina, with her husband.